Swarf

Swarf

Chris Kinsey

Published 2011 by
Smokestack Books
PO Box 408, Middlesbrough TS5 6WA
e-mail : info@smokestack-books.co.uk
www.smokestack-books.co.uk

Swarf
Chris Kinsey
Copyright 2011, by Chris Kinsey, all rights reserved
Cover image: Chris Kinsey
Cover photographs: Liz Hinkley

Printed by
EPW Print & Design Ltd

ISBN 978-0-9564175-2-7
Smokestack Books gratefully
acknowledges the support of
Arts Council England

Smokestack Books is
represented by Inpress Ltd
www.inpressbooks.co.uk

For Evan and Liz and in memory of my father Jakob Reynen.

Thanks are due to the editors of the following publications, where some of these poems first appeared: *Avocado, Coffee House Poetry, Dream Catcher, Envoi, Eyewear, iota,* Todd Swift and Val Stevenson (eds) *In the Criminal's Cabinet, Lavender Review, Neon Highway, New Welsh Review, Nthposition, Poetry 2000 Competition Anthology Kent and Sussex Poetry Society, Poetry Nottingham,* Esther Morgan (ed) *Reactions 3, Pen&inc at UEA, Roundyhouse, Smiths Knoll, Smoke, Tears in the Fence, The Ver Prize 2007, The Yellow Crane. Currents* was joint winner of Ledbury Poetry Festival's first *Always be a Poet* competition. In 2008 the river poems were performed by Montgomeryshire Youth Theatre and Vox Orbis Choir in Theatr Clera and Oriel Davies Gallery.

Contents

- 11 Getting to Know the Greyhound
- 13 Hunters
- 14 Incident at Cricieth
- 15 Currents – Market Day
- 16 October Streaming
- 17 Overheard in Aberystwyth
- 19 Downstream
- 20 Swinging
- 21 Cabbage Whites
- 25 Flight Practice
- 26 Dead White Stick
- 27 Joe's Challenge
  - Chemistry Lessons
  - Vocation
  - Confession 1969
  - Kung Fu 2008.
- 30 Writing Coursework
- 34 Self Defence
- 35 Boxing Gloves
- 36 Meeting Pam Again
- 37 Salvage
- 38 In the Forests of the Night
- 39 Neighbours
- 40 From the Back of the Bus
- 41 Fishophile
- 42 Breach of the Peace
- 43 Fags & Hairspray
- 44 At the Gym
- 45 Butt
- 46 *It's Not Even Mad Friday*
- 47 Heroes
- 48 Immigrants
- 50 Not Superstitious
- 51 Evening Shift after Bad News

- 52 Dandelions
- 53 Quilt
- 54 Looking for Billy
- 55 Someone's handed me this casket
- 56 The End of Visiting
  - Snowflakes
  - Firn
  - Ice Field
  - Niche
  - Periglacial
- 59 Out of Hospital
- 60 Toads Revisited, Revisited
- 61 Zip
- 62 Service User
- 63 Vacant Plots
- 64 Watching the Window-Cleaner
- 65 Sighting
- 66 Cleaning Norwich Millennium Library Roof
- 67 Flint
- 68 Lucky Dip
- 69 Dust
- 70 On Sitting by the Blue Stove
- 71 The River's Sneaking Low
- 72 Whooper Swans
- 73 Sunday Shoes
- 74 Tortoiseshells at Lydbury North
- 75 Greyhound Separation Anxieties

Getting to Know the Greyhound

The slightest sniff makes your muscles ripple.
Squirrels set you arrow-alert
then you soften and move like quicksand.

A kingfisher flies low, close to the bank.
Overtaking its reflection, it falters
on a spillage of turquoise.

The turquoise walks off the water
flutters into a wrap-around skirt.
A wolf-whistle shrills afternoon silent.

'What a beaut!'
You reel back, hide from the man
with noughts and crosses on his neck.

'Ex-racer? – Winner?'
'Don't know her history,
only had her a fortnight.'

'Bet she's a good rabbiter.'
Coaxing you from behind my legs,
we walk on. He calls,

'Can I have pups off of her?'
Nodding at the pram I say,
'You'll have to stick to babies.'

The woman grins, but he frowns.
'She's been spayed.' I say.
'Shame – if I had a pup

I wouldn't do nothing cruel –
just a bit of lamping.
Gotta feed these two!'

Loosed for the first time, you rip
through ripe grasses, stand crook-pawed
as rabbits white-tail into hard earth.

I open my arms and call with all my lungs.
You're instantly in my shadow's pool
pressing like a strong current.

Hunters

Released early, I track where lurchers and terriers
nose between maisonettes and out-houses,
slide sideways through a gap in the fence
to a world held secret by the school-room's glass.

Every glimpse made variations on Brueghel's
Hunters in the Snow. Now I enter the scene,
walk diagonally down a slope,
shoulders hunched under a back-pack of books.

I miss my own deep-chested hounds.
They'd charge a fluttering leaf
into the willow thicket where pheasants
shed coppers and gold.

Without dogs I'm shifty, looking over my shoulder,
up through the candelabras of horse-chestnuts
to a magpie's solitary arc.
I get fussy about snow in my boots

tramping this barbed line between Powis Castle Park
and housing estate. Looking back
on a molehill fortified with vodka bottles,
I discover a short-cut to the supermarket.

Incident at Cricieth

'One day I am thinking of a color: orange.'
(Frank O'Hara)

Orange is the last thing on my mind
on this cold-sweat day.
Fog smothers the bay, holds
the sea close to shore.
White waves rule, blunting headlands.
By Blackrock the train window is streaked with rain.
On the platform, scruffed by damp,
I tell myself a heavy bag and the chill
are insufficient reasons to sag.
Boys too young for the pub
thud a football on the vacant car-park.
Their goal is the Ladies.

I climb to main street –
most shops have no intention of opening before
February. As I turn to investigate being caught
by a wire claw, I'm in a fairground cascade.
Seville oranges catapult from their crate
faster than I can compute cause and effect.
Before I can stoop to grasp two in open-pored skins,
a surge of young men, full of good jeer,
juggle them back to the blond, splintery crate.
The moment is re-set, leaving me
considering bubbling shred and pulp,
wondering how much zest will spread.

At breakfast time I pick up Frank O'Hara,
'I write a line
about orange. Pretty soon it is a
whole page of words....'

Currents

No more echoing screams, no greasy thrills,
all the bright vans, and pulsing lights
of the funfair struck overnight.

Across town, the pens of the cattle market
were razed. Tesco built fast under arc lights.
Yesterday was Grand Opening.

On the bridge, a man, smart-for-town
stares down at the stony shallows,
leans uncomfortably far over ferry-gliding ducks.

Others are leaning too, they list into air
thickening with cross-hatching snow.
The last gentleman's outfitters is going slowly:

Viyella reduced, checked caps half price.
Currys is clearing out too.
The Seconds Shop went months ago.

Walking on through the shrinking street market,
a muscle in my back is a little too tight,
not painful, but tense enough to pull me out-of-true.

When I return, the man is still leaning over the bridge,
grainy behind snowflakes and blurred by cloud.
Someone lobs a three-quarters ciggy from a van

and he snaps into focus, snatching it before it dampens.
'That's better.' He smiles and goes,
leaving a gap for the wind's harmonics.

Cries get louder. A lone goose flies close to the hill's rim
unpicking the seam where weather fronts merge. It beats
for its flock and cold down falls.

Market Day 23 February 2010

October Streaming

Sunlight tilts like a plane's wing
through leaves just starting to stream
and Midas grass that's tender fresh
after summer's scorching.

Cherry trees launch crimson leaf-boats
into the river's racing currents.
It's warm enough to sit by rapids
watching whirlpools write themselves out
hoping for a salmon to leap.

A neon dart streaks from black lace
river-roots – the kingfisher
shrugging rainbows – steals thoughts
with turquoise and delays the darkness.

Overheard in Aberystwyth

November evening – everything's half-hearted,
ambivalent, but the wind has stopped.
In the deli a woman wipes the cheese wire,
removes oranges from the juicer
and polishes its nozzles - the tapas bar is open.

It's Chef's night off,
he's sitting on a high stool drinking
Spanish beer talking to an Australian couple
about how he came here to be with a woman who died.
He asks why they're so far from home.

We're going wherever the wind blows.
'We had a gust of 91mph here yesterday.
Blew the sea over the bandstand.
You wouldn't believe it today.'
No, not that calm little bay?

Tell me, how do you catch your sea-bass out there?
'With a live prawn.'
And how do you catch your live prawn?
'Dip for them in rock pools.'
I've been lucky with these new soft gel lures.

*It's not the movement through the water
that attracts, but the disturbance of the sand
when they land.
That's what makes the fish pounce.
Do you go for your bass in a boat?*

'No, we take a line off the foreshore,
cast into the breaking surf –
the rocks here help us:
the sea-bass line up in the channels to feed.
Best to go at night.'

It's all a bit new to me.
Before I washed-up here
I'd only fished inland lakes and the Trent,
coarse fishing –
I'm more of a carp man than sea-bass.'

Downstream

The roof ridge splits
rain-strike to run-off,
droplets explode under streetlights.

'There'll be plenty of salmon
running the river tonight,
riding high in this.'

I picture the brown Severn,
just yards from the door,
swelling silver with spawning fish.

'That one I nearly got you twenty years ago
was a magnificent red cock-fish
hanging clear in the current.

I knew I could have him,
but my fingers were so cold
I just couldn't knot the snap-hook.

Barry came by so I asked him to tie it
and I cast. The fish took the bait -
vanished upstream.

Barry's smirk rippled,
'All the fish
in this stretch are mine!"

Swinging

'Push me.

    Higher.

        Faster!'

I fling you onto air.

You swing between now and the future.

The biggest push raises you high
over playground shouts –
next term you'll be down there.

I pivot between now and then -

a summer holiday singing Beatles songs
soaking-up grown-up's gossip
and being sworn to secrecy.

'How do we stop?'

I catch the pendulum,
lift you down.

Almost in tears you cry,

*'Oh no,
I've got holding-on hands.'*

Curling my hot, holding-back hands around,
I stroke them open
and hold one tight.

Cabbage Whites

I

Teatimes, my play is shushed -
T.V. screens blaze with napalm
Buddhist monks sit robed in flame.

Daytimes I crawl under cabbages,
their hidden heads chin me
into earth dry as scabs.

Lying low,
watching caterpillars fret the canopy,
I pluck one,
stare into huge eyes,
play it like a puppy.

It squirts. I flick.

It dangles then hauls its hunger
back to gorge leaf.

I wish I could grow that fast.

Squirming free,
I chase ragged flight

till I'm stuck under the windowsill
fingering the hard case of a chrysalis
feeling the struggle in its tip.

II

Stretching my tallest, I grab
the brindled knob,
push its whisper of release
into darkness.

The shed door shudders on concrete.
I squeeze past my doll's pram,
spring onto the bench,
take command of the top shelf.

Pop bottles sparkle - turps, paraffin, meths.
Striking notes with my bamboo wand,
I conjure flames.
In the storm dead butterflies glide
and whirl into dust heaps.

I've just prised the lid off paint
a voice calls -

I'm down, crushing slack,
wrenching the tell-tale door.
The word *nothing* ready to fly.

III

After dinner dad leads me back to the shed.

I close my eyes against forensics;
anthracite footprints,
my fingerprints streaking dangerous bottles.

I hold my breath.
He pushes a golden syrup tin into my hands
and cycles back to the forge.

'Clear all the caterpillars for me.'

I treasure unicorns, lions, crowns,
trace the tin's white scrolls.

Caterpillars beat against its bottom.
Sweat trickles as I bend to clear each leaf.

I shake those that have risen,
seal them with a gentle press.

A halo of white butterflies graces me.
some drink me and fly
to make the only clouds.

IV

The opened shed is my laboratory.

My hands unscrew bottles
mix cocktails,
pour pink paraffin
down shiny sides.

Green and gold skins blush,
heads rear, bodies pulse,
jive, magnify, shrink -

it's swimming baths and fairground mirrors.

I see I have made them drown.

V

Darting indoors,
I ransack my mother's bag.

Underneath wads of lip-printed tissue
I feel the rough edge of a box, rattle it.

Holding the struck match over the tin until it curls

I let go.

There's a gasp of nothing happening,
nothing, then flames brighter than in stoves
wilder than the flames dad holds
over steels to make them glow.

I've no mask or shield -
they hiss, spit, lick at me.

Skins split.

I shove the torch away
run down banks
shelling molehills, startling cattle.

Scuffed shingle scatters like shot
when I plunge into the river.

I wade until I'm somersaulting for air.

VI

Speechless, dad ushers me
past the charred tin's mass grave,
pays silver into my shivering hands.

Before he leads me to a scalding bath
I cover the dead with rose petals
and grass cuttings.

Soot and grit mark my tide.

I think of wings smudging my hands.

Ghostly with too much talc,
I emerge into the 6 o'clock news.

Flight Practice

Sudden jet-scream tears the air,
spilling thoughts.

Thrust back into the chair,
my conscripted breath

gasps the engines clear of the hill.

What's held in ignites -

Free-falling in burning fuselage

breath expires

roars fade.

A blackbird's already singing all-clear
loud and liquid from the hazels.

Dead White Stick

A lightning strike
washed up on a beach -

prised from the teeth of playing dogs
to conduct leaps, growls, snap-gymnastics.

Everyone strokes down its grain into stories.
Shape-shifting it to:

water serpents, a diviner's rod,
an olive branch,

an antler from a rutting stag,
unicorn horn, campfire crackle.

Sunk skulls with eye-sockets
crying scorched sand.

Pips spit the broadcaster into announcing
the first bombing raids on Baghdad.

It rakes its way out of my bag,
to fork at the moon in its oily halo.

19 March 2003

Joe's Challenge

'Your job, as a poet is to make things better. I bet you could make something out of this sucked-out drink carton.'

I   **Chemistry Lessons**

Focusing on experiments cancels time
so I'm fourteen again too -
just won a battle to take Science
not Domestic Science,
I'm excited by crystals,
in my element with *The Periodic Table*.
Polysyllables play in my mouth
like bubble gum:
Polythene, Polyvinyl chloride, Polyester.

I'm glad to get my hands on apparatus:
beakers, dragon-powered Bunsen burners,
rubber bungs, clinking racks of test-tubes,
steaming chemicals: anhydrous copper sulphate,
fresh green ferrous sulphate, flowers of sulphur.
Off to the fume cupboard to make hydrogen sulphide.
The craze for stink bombs distracts our teacher.
We spill mercury, herd globules
along grooves in the bench,
dribble it down our Life and Love lines.

We dare to lift the crucible lid
and stare into magnesium's glare.
I fall in love with valency, volatility,
with symbols: Hg. Mg. Ag. Al – Aluminium,
connect to Geography – the location of industries,
bauxite, hydro-electricity, smelting.
I stick to my stool in awe -
atmospheric pressure crumples a gallon can
as water vapour drives off the inner air.
The Tate and Lyle lion tumbles from its tripod.

II Vocation

Mum fed fresh loaves to the new slicer,
I checked each wrapper's flap for a firm seal,
ran curls of white wax under my fingernail.
I'd longed to score the cuticles
of succulent spears: sansevieria, bitter aloe, ice plants.

Back at school we hid in the chapel to escape the wind,
watched candle-flicker gild white walls
and Easter lilies sterilize the altar.
I looked shiftily for a patron saint of wonder
in natural forms and selection.

III Confession 1969

I bought a sheath knife with my first earnings,
and caused consternation in school.
My headmistress said, 'She's not
going to hurt anyone.'

I kept it for whittling sticks,
flicking muck from horses' hooves,
teased my thumb along the blade
to teach it tenderness.

IV Kung Fu 2008

My first time with a steel sword,
I hold the hilt in a loose grip,
the thrill is all in perfecting control
practising a parry in slow-motion,
an ulna-over-radius deflection
of my opponent's blade without
a slip or a scrape.

It's a conductor to draw my spirit
out beyond the dragons fighting

over my centre. I direct my focus
to a still point beyond arm's length.
The slow turn around the thumb
releases the catch on held breath.

Writing Coursework

'Boxing is a barbarous activity which has no place in today's civilised society.' Discuss.

Round I

You sit with a spread of print-outs,
shuffle pages, make the calculation
that boxing has been popular
for six thousand and nine years,
then write your introduction,
as the bell goes.

Round II

In out,
you click on fancy fonts,
make letters grow bold
and shrink

In out. In out,
like a tongue,
it pokes from your tee shirt sleeve
as you guide your mouse.

In or out?
I decide to come out with it,
'That's one hell of a bruise.
Did someone grab your arm?'

In out,
You snort and flush.
*Do you honestly think **anyone**
could give me this with just a grab?*

In out.
Feel it. Feel the dents.
Some kid called Darren jumped me
wearing an illegal knuckleduster.

In out. In out.
Fists jabbed. *He tried*
to hit me in the head.
We rub our temples tenderly.

Up down.
'You did well to block.'
You find your next paragraph, type out:
How does boxing differ from street fighting?

Round III

Every time you want relief from the chore of writing
you say, *I reckon you could be a good little boxer.*

I admit to a bit of Karate in my twenties,
still practise a little defensive Kung Fu,
but I haven't told you what happened when Mr Thomas
came from the A stream to teach us boxing.

Aged nine, Class Nine - I was chosen
to throw the first punch. Pumped on pride
but wary of the boys' simmering scorn
I struck above the belt.

My favourite teacher staggered
through the ring of classmates
to land winded on the stove-guard
rattling our crate of free school milk.

Shaking, I apologized,
flooded with relief
when he unbent to gasp,
Your trouble is you don't realize your strength.

Mum said this to dad when we sparred.
I could never hammer
his invincible blacksmith power
or dent his anvil guard.

Round IV

I haven't told you, either, why
I stopped wearing sandals at seventeen –

all to do with a sentimental drunk
losing his beat
swaying out of control
and treading on my toes.

First lesson in Anger Management:
Always wear protective toe caps.

Round V

You work with great concentration.
I think about Rocky Marciano.

Suddenly, you drum on the desk
making the soundtrack to

Eye of the Tiger,
a hit so long before you were born

you don't know how you know the tune.
We swagger out of class singing

*It's the eye of the tiger, it's the thrill of the fight
Risin' up to the challenge of our rival.*

Round VI

As you type your conclusion,
I watch a poppy strip in the heat.

Afterwards, I pick up two wilting petals -
red bruising to black near the stem,

press them and plan the lesson
we still need to have on the delicacy

of blood vessels, brain tissue -
all the mystery of who we are

packed into a cranium smaller
than a 10 ounce boxing glove.

Self-Defence

So much depends
upon

an exact tilt
of the pelvis –

being able to torque the torque

and balance a smile.

Boxing Gloves

Handed to me for amnesty –

these veterans pucker on the shelf
like a couple who've
taken their teeth out to be comfortable.

Blood-burst red,
the outer skin's soft
as the skin over fontanelles.

The linings' shredded strings
are a clench on the throat tendons
of the boy conscript you silenced.

Punch-drunk on sweat,
the innards couldn't absorb
the shock or knock the replays cold.

Putting them on's a fumble into
puppet darkness

a scrabble back
into the foxhole of a Falklands spring –

the shock of ripping awake from a garrotte

your best mate shrieking bayonet steel.

Meeting Pam Again

'I'm still here
I'm walking
I'm not in a wheelchair.

I come round
in the octopus arms of nurses.
Had to fight them all the way to the toilet.

I said, 'You're not having me
On no effing bedpan.'
Fought them all the way.

I always was a fighter.
Got my car licence back.
Coming off disability in April.

A lot of my memory's come back too
and you're in there –
part of my history.

I still make silly mistakes.
But sometimes I can catch a word
by moving my arm and writing on the air.'

Salvage

'Those masterful images because complete
Grew in pure mind, but out of what began?
A mound of refuse or the sweepings of a street,
Old kettles, old bottles, and a broken can...' (W. B. Yeats)

Week 13

There's a lull in the lesson
and he says, 'You're passionate
about your poetry, aren't you?
It's like me and cars.'

I think about
the thrill of reckless imagery
and the way I t.w.o.c.
things people say.

Week 14

'You work hellish hard at all this writing –
do you ever get paid for it?'

'I've just banked a cheque for £200
for some poems.'

He scales down his scowl to be polite.
'If you saved all your dog food tins

crushed 'em and took 'em
to Lovatt's scrapyard

you'd soon get yourself
two hundred quid.'

In the Forests of the Night

Upholstered in studs and steel,
initials inked into his own grained bark,
he kills the chainsaw whine,
rides the ruts home to chase
the dragon and tend his bonsai trees.

Neighbours

'Why'd'I push him?

'Cause he kep'
on and on

Nasty little two-stroke dirt bike

Sounded like a hornet
buzzing
inside me head

When I went out
he was on *my* dirt
in *my* wallflowers doing wheelies.

If he'd had a four-stroke
and kept the revs down.
it mighta been different

From the Back of the Bus

'D'you see the Tae Kwon Do lot
in the paper winning prizes?

I tell you it's hellish different
than when we done it.

Shit, I hope this bus isn't late –
I'm meeting the missus.

Only met her on Friday night,
she's hellish smart, hellish tall.

How old d'you reckon she is?
She's only fucking fifteen.

I thought whoa, hang on a minute –
then I thought, what's four years?

She's coming with me for a blood test.
They think I've got diabetes.

I tell you, I can't be arsed with none
of that injecting needles and stuff.

Needles go right through me.'

Fishophile

You're a sad bastard Colin
sitting there all unshaven in your B.O.
getting turned on by fish.
You're a fishophile.
Don't tell me you're not –
Fishophile!

The rest of us called up this real cool site, right,
with beautiful women in bikinis,
then, this guy walks past 'em
carrying a great big bloody fish,
and Colin comes to life and says,
'Cor, how big d'you think that one is?'

He's all turned on by the fucking fish.
Don't tell me you weren't turned on, Colin.
I saw the boner taking off from your pants
like a 747 and now you trawl the web
looking for sites of fish.
You're a sad bastard Colin.

Breach of the Peace

A hailstorm sweeps the street again.

Under a rainbow, outside Spar,
a gang of girls toss their heads
and duel in text messages.

The lone cop cruises,
a white flag of chip papers
muffles his grill.

He slides his window down,
'Keep the noise down girls.
It's Sunday after all!'

Silence -
except for the kiss of rubber sealing glass.

The girls wait.

The drive-on player exits.

'Fuck Sunday!' ricochets
off every plate glass window.

Fags & Hairspray

After the tour of the scabs and the skin graft
there's silence.

We sit still, mulling the rumours.

'Tell us what *really* happened?'

'I was worn-out
visiting mum in hospital
twice a day for three weeks....'

The words chafe,
disintegrate into coughs.

'Mum's friend offered to go
so I had a bath and lay on the bed.

Woke up late, hair helluva a mess,
sorted it with hairspray,
went to the toilet, lit a fag -

Never come round for five days.

When I did, tubes up my nose
went right down my throat.
I didn't realise and yanked them -

I haven't been this fucking hoarse
since going to see Bruce Springsteen.'

At the Gym

I'm rowing like a galley slave.
Gina and Sue cycle;
going nowhere fast.
Instead we get a tour of tattoos:

'The Teletubbies are for the twins.
Eli chose the small heart.
I'm having Winnie The Pooh done for Kylie.
No more room; so no more kids - best birth control!'

Gina nods and pants.
Every time she pedals
a pod of dolphins ride a billow of buttock
and plunge back.

Butt

Just found out why
my boots are called:
'Yeeha!'

Nothing to do with line dancing
or spinning silver spurs –

Everything to do with ice
grooming road metal

and the brow of a 1:4 hill
putting it's head down
to buck.

It's Not Even Mad Friday

Reality's taken down its name plaque.
The door marked, *This door must be shut
properly at all times,* finally is -
nothing, on this street paved with gold,
but me and the wind bossing old leaves.

Warehouse walls start to warp and shudder,
A taxi slews round the corner
and it's empty - driverless empty -
running on *Down Town* with Petula Clark
blaring, *Where all the lights are gay*

louder than the Sixties. Right on cue,
it screeches to the lights, shakes its boot
and turns pink. Beyond Belisha beacons
a disability scooter bangs the kerb shouting,
'Someone's stolen my daughter.'

Heroes

You can guarantee the real serious jobs
come through in the small hours of Saturday,
that's when most healthy people get killed.
I try to get a kip while the other drivers are working
just in case.

The last heart transplant bloke I had,
was too poorly to talk so I turned on the radio.
D'you know?
Every song I hopped to went on about the heart.

I switched it off.

No end need bone marrow, you know?
I've had a call three times to be a donor,
95, 96, 97% match so far.
Not quite enough -

I just think of John Wayne
keeping going with cancer
and I keep telling myself:
'Pain is just a word.
Pain is just a word.'

Immigrants

Mesmerised by the squish of wipers,
tyres, door suctions,
I haven't kept time.

Stratford Road is one long rule -
pet shops and post offices
mark distance.

I must be getting close.

The man beside me relaxes;
all the rivers on his coat
change course.

When the drip falls from his nose
I ask directions.

With deft handwork he cuts
major junctions out of the fug,
counts off traffic lights and bus-stops.

I'm unsure of number,
his English struggles with names
and landmarks I don't know.

Shrugging, he smiles
I'll show you.

*Gotta bus pass see
won't cost me nothing.*

He points through window mist,
Sparkhill park, very nice.
I lose track in all the trickles.

Free day today
Free day tomorrow
he chants against the pelican
crossing's urgency.

I surprise myself
and ask what he does,
Welder, factory worker.

He turns his collar up
leans against the return stop.

Thanking him

I think about my father
standing over spark showers,
saturdays too,

coming home deaf and ragged,
swarf in his soles
scraping like spent shrapnel.

Did you make enough welds
to fuse your *heimweh*?

And what do you hear
now that anvils are still?

Not Superstitious

On a day of single magpies,
the cloud with the silver lining
is all set to discharge.

Evening Shift after Bad News

Diagnosis drops down like a hood.
I'm a sundowner drifting into The Pines at supper time
but, tonight, Terry treats me like a guest
and ushers me to the place he's laid.
He toasts me with golden juice.
Braced for acid orange – I smile at sweet mango.

After the meal, other tenants and staff go out.
He flicks the tea towel like a matador, goads me
into washing up. We charge the clean up,
cheer our reflections in copper-bottomed pans.
He roars the fridge open, seizes gold sealed kippers
like a trophy. We put them back before the stars of butter
melt.

In the lounge, he takes control of the T.V.
There's a shoot-out in Soap Land. Terry's up
toe-to-toeing it with the gunman, remonstrating,
'No, no, don't do it!'

The credits roll so I point upstairs,
mime taking a shower. He goes without protest.

When the others return, I'm free to go.
Filling in my time sheet, I write: Relief Support
and wonder who, on this shift, has the real claim?

Dandelions

They walk the garden path arm in arm,
his old taunt drifts back
with late summer's downy seeds.

You're as strong as a lion

Even as she braced herself for the tease
pride made her strong.

a dandelion.

She hurled herself against his iron arms
fierce as a cub.

Then, she only knew the hollow leaves,
stems that popped milkily at the plucking
and the dizzy clocks that blew.

Now, she sees every parachute
is tipped with a chisel to widen
the cracks in his path.

She has seen roots buckle tarmac
slough off roads, pavements, airstrips
and leads him back inside.

Quilt

A lifetime's scraps of blue saved in a bag.

I craft time with rag and template,
folding every raw-edged piece,
trimming, padding.

When daylight fails
I plot pain into a star,
many pointed, sore.

My needle,
pushing warp and weft,
bobs the final journey.

Each stitch is a sigh.
Each knot ties anger.
When you fall asleep

I snip the thread.

Looking for Billy

It came on suddenly
this blindness thing

like walking into the barn
on a Summer day –

split shafts, shadows,
shapes.

Thought he was mucking about
Hide 'n' seeking me.

Thought it was my eyes playing tricks
when I found him,

but it wasn't a feedbag
rocking from the rafters.

His father went to the War
brought back a darkness.

Billy caught it.

Now the dark's in me.

Bits of me come back sometimes –

I'm going to look for Billy.

Someone's handed me this casket

but I don't want cool, porous, clay,
I want to cup a head,
a bottom, feel a kick,
swim in your unfocused smile.

I can't lift this lid,
undo grasping fingers,
scatter the ashes of future footsteps
and silent shouts.

The mobile stirs above your cot.

The End of Visiting

I   Snowflakes

Evening develops like an X-ray
on the ward's window –
no diagnosis.

I leave you with some snowdrops
you say, *They*
smell of home.

II   Firn

Hands stinging with *Spirigel,*

I join other visitors herded by nurses.
Too agitated for the lift, I spring down the caged stairs,

ignore signs for: Main Exit, Chapel, League of Friends,
dare down deeper in search of a short-cut.

My lungs vacuum in terror of viruses, radiation,
masked surgeons, scalpels, sutures.

Like peristalsis, the bustle of purpose
propels me service-side. In the tricky

tunnel behind the kitchens I shrink.
The giant Perspex and rubber door slides and seals.

Dodging pallets and ringing gas-cylinders,
I leap from the loading bay

to the sharpness of frost.

III   Ice Field

Outside, four o'clock is boy's hour.

Sick of the spatter of slush and ice shrapnel,
three of them give up on the football pitch
and kick a ball hard against the mortuary wall.
It rebounds and reverberates; one of them shouts,
Hey, what's that song From Full Metal Jacket?
The others chant straight into: *I don't know but I've been told
Eskimo fanny's mighty cold.*

They fall into line, march off behind the leader.
The truism of the refrain, their side of puberty,
makes me smile. I follow the parade away
from the smoking incinerator, ship's funnel
to a scream of landlocked gulls, until
they slip silently through a garden fence
and I shrug under cedars brushing off ice.

At the bus stop, paper-boys converge to practise skids.
Slush from their back tyres arcs and spills.
Rust from the emerging weighbridge stains the snow.

IV   Niche

I've defaulted to my school setting
and sat in the seat over the back wheel.

It seems moments, not decades, since I was there
with you waving from the building site.

On cold mornings, if you threw a brick too enthusiastically,
frost stripped the skin off your palm.

On the field trip to identify glacial features,
we passed your lodgings in the remains of *Lake Blakemere*.

Now, you lie bleeding on the bed of *Lake Lapworth*
still I can't stop the flow.

As I head for the shelter of hills
I think about the laws of thermodynamics.

V   Periglacial

Sunrise is cold enough to clear time,
and re-cast hills as cooling volcanoes.
The river's molten under a flame sky.

Returning geese draw an arrow
east – west
to the clamouring present.

Schoolboys send a bag spinning
to the centre of a flood pane-
it's thin ice after all.

Out of Hospital

Release sets you fluttering on your own force.
You hover a beat or two
then your balance breaks.

Stepping to steady you, I catch your arm,
hold you upright in a brief embrace.

Your pulse is whirring,
your heart
a trapped wren.

Dazed wasps and bees drone
most flowers are gone or gummed
with dew.

October leaves streak the grass
with last brightness.

Your stare blinks off a daisy
you point and slur, *'My words
scattered all across the wet field.'*

Toads Revisited, Revisited

Walking around in the park
is better than work -
people you meet of an afternoon,
hearing the hours chime

knowing they must go to kitchens,
wait at tables, set off to call centres
where the customers need counselling
but the company wants quick orders.

Goths in long coats must shed them at tills.
All of them dodging the toad work
by making the most of the river,
the sunshine, the grass to lie on.

A carer swaps the scent of wet sheets
for lime flowers and blushing roses.
A mother stoops to wheel the bike
her child will wobble home on.

Turning over failures by the river rapids
another can of Tennant's *psssts* -
'She's stopped taking her medication.'
What else can I answer?

But listen, look at the cans
deep in the litter-basket,
and say, 'Give me your arm, old toad,
let's stagger down Boundary Road.'

Zip

The carer's Ford is running rich
on minimum wage and rally-romance.

He tips John out too soon,
guns the throttle and is gone.

'Bloody awful day yesterday.'
I agree, replaying floods and mudslides.

The shelter has condensation on the run,
but there's no sign of a bus.

Over our canopy,
a rainbow arches its back.

Neither of us shifts - the pot of gold
is spent on hazels and small coin birches.

And it's enough, in November,
for colour to come to pastures and skies.

The wind that shrank the river overnight
makes us white-fingered,

'Will you fasten my coat please?'
Genuflecting to get his zip on track

I smile to think how this must look.

But we have met often enough
to make zip teeth mesh into a grin.

Service User

Why are the staff -
Always in meetings?

Always jibber-jabber?
     Jibber-jabber?
Always problems,
     problems?
Always bad moments?
Always bickering?

Why can't people -
Just talk sense?

Vacant Plots

Rain animates the world beyond the glass.
Bare twigs sprout a crop of the fattest drops
water can hold, silvery as spoons
lining up on the draining-board.

Bullfinches ripen the empty apple trees.
Boundary yews shrug in seclusion,
shrubs huddle all borders. My thoughts too,
are screened, trained to a tenant's need.

At home my gazing's different.
The garden's a runway to buzzard spirals,
vapour-trail ciphers. At doves' ovations
I wait for word-specks to form.

Watching the Window-Cleaner

He's nearly top-rung
up where heat shimmers –
a wash-cloth cowboy in a big red hat.

The eagle inked into his forearm
soars to become a buzzard,
slowly lassoing thermals.

As he polishes reflections on the glass flank
his muscles ride the great plains
of articulation –

I name them like a herd:
deltoids, rhomboids, trapezius.

He thinks about hanging up the chamois,
saddling the dormer,
riding the ridge tiles as a roofer.

Sighting

We turn our backs
on window-shopping and sales
walk away from town.

Seven drakes, heads and necks
green from dipping the depths,
scull the slow bend.

A willow leans from pale chippings.
Old saw wounds are a quiver
of amber arrows.

At a gap in the alders
the weir makes water back flip.
We watch stones grow beards.

A whistle shrills us heron-still.
Before we tune to its signal
our eyes see a dart so swift

the beak pierces from turquoise flights,
draws us to our toes.
It pauses on a branch,

but the branch is a fired bow.
River-rush erases colours,
ripples make us squint and doubt.

Cleaning Norwich Millennium Library Roof

Two men stand on islands in sky
and bridge the strait with broom staves.

Co-ordinating push, pull and dip,
they sweep particulates from the lenses.

Cloud-dammed blue floods in.
The library stacks are tanks of light.

A seagull, seeing his chance,
mounts his reflection in slow motion.

The atrium's curve slides him like slush,
then, in a fury of wings,

he rises,
soars over a perfect image.

Flint

(after Wallace Stevens)

'And nothing need be explained,'
said the stone,
sea-spittle drying.

Not knapped,
nor chipped
to blade or arrowhead.

Not struck for sparks
nor saved for slingshot,
but fingered

out of a shingle bed
and cradled in a palm,
on a morning where gulls,

whiter than Sizewell's vanishing globe,
nestle into footprints
the crunch has walked from.

Lucky Dip

I pass the bag.

Sam's first to pick.

'May I keep the stone?'

My fingers start to clamour
Finders keepers; losers weepers.
but I quell them.

His voice is hoarse,
fades into breaths.

'I used to have my travelling stone -

Gave it away.

Now I sit in the house
four or five days at a stretch.'

His thumb and palm caress the pebble
till it's warm as the thrush egg
he says he fondled as a boy.

'I sit in the chair so long
can't walk straight
down the street after.

Look, the stone's got a birthmark -'

'An arrow,' she says.

'*No*. It's a swallow.
May I keep this stone?'

Dust

After the river
I lived in the road,
trickled stones through a drain grating
heard riddles of splash and echo.

As sparrows bathed,
fanning smoke without fire,
I tasted again
river without rain.

On Sitting by the Blue Stove

Humdrum
          is the fridge,
less tight-lipped than it should be,
thrumming me drowsy.

Stove heat griddles thoughts,
riddles flesh and feeling
casts me square asleep.

I wake, feet in fluff,
strapped straight by cobwebs,
open-mouthed before the washer.

Stupor
          is what's for supper.

The River's Sneaking Low

On the one deep, slow, bend,
the shallows shush
and the sleeping moon bobs.

Whooper Swans

Woken by cries –
I sift cloud-fill for shape, for form,
think geese -

        see swans
catch colour from streaks of snow
tacking the Arctic down latitudes.

A bugling pair head straight-necked up the Severn,
land where dilute sun and flood-silt
sprout winter-wheat.

Silent as relict snowdrifts, the grazing flock
waits for thaw's eviction.
Pumlumon raises a white brow over the source.

Sunday Shoes

When church preached its sacred mysteries
I always thought of dad's shoes and his shed.
Polished, light tan, Sunday best shoes –
so unlike his work boots,
sooty toecaps nicked with steel scars
like miniature domes of night sky,
oily with Wren's Liquid Dubbin,

I didn't realise, when I snatched the packet
from a Woolworth's spike and helped to officiate
the Stick-a-sole ceremony, that I, too, was being prepared.
I roughed each leather sole with a wire brush,
resisted the urge to bite the shiny rubber soles
that would coat his tread like liquorice whirls.
I stood back when he hammered segs into heels and toes,
clamoured to have them on my shoes so I could stride,
and strike sparks, though he was at pains to silence his.
When he knelt to pray, I thought the silver crescents
a gift from the patron saint of Blacksmiths.

The strong glue set me tracking the Holy Spirit
to the shelves of the shed: to White Spirit
and Esso Blue, aromatic liquids with volatile halos,
violet Meths the colour of Lent vestments.
Was the Feast of Pentecost done
with sneaky flicks of cigarette lighters?
I sampled 3 in 1 oil as it suckled my bike chain
and prepared for the grace of sensation,
the sacrament of words. Later, I relished Hopkins:
All things counter, original, spare, strange:
because I trusted his *ooze of oil crushed.*

Those tan shoes outlasted my churchgoing.

Tortoiseshells at Lydbury North

Church-shy, I'm drawn from shivering
amongst graves and the surplices of snowdrops
to the plain page of the south transept.

Curious, not for names on a register,
or details of the ceremony, just for
a sense of where my grandparents married.

Lattice light, candles and Christmas roses,
all blanched like vellum. I lift a latch
and discover stairs to the school-room.

Casual as confetti, small tortoiseshell wings
scatter oak steps. Scraps of torn manuscript -
one side charred and brown, the other

illuminated with summer: mimulus,
nasturtium, ink spots, borders
filled with lunules of speedwell.

I speculate on their fall:
kindled from hibernation by winter sun,
a wild, fast fluttering, flames spiralling upwards

beating against glass traps until starved and exhausted,
they dropped to a flicker, ticking like snow striking slate,
stopped in a papery, ashy hush.

Greyhound Separation Anxieties

I   London

Arrive Euston,
dump bag in a cheap hotel,
head straight for the Charing Cross Road.

In every book shop
interrupt courses of poetry
with centre page spreads of greyhounds.

II   Cardiff

11.30 p.m.
stuck to the betting shop window
calling to number 3
in the life-sized racing photo.

III   Bardsey

In dreams forbidden dogs
bound down the mountain,
race the narrows
leap the black rocks behind the lighthouse.

Waking
my voice is hoarse
and my brand new sleeping bag
full of fine black hairs.

IV   Aberystwyth

Faced with a long night
in the back room of a B&B
I buy James Kelman's
Greyhound for Breakfast.